RESPONSIBLE GUN OWNERSHIP

Handguns

Safety, Selection, and Use

By John Cashin

ELDORADO INK

Eldorado Ink
PO Box 100097
Pittsburgh, PA 15233
www.eldoradoink.com

Produced by OTTN Publishing, Stockton, New Jersey

CPSIA compliance information: Batch#RGO2014-1.
For further information, contact Eldorado Ink at info@eldoradoink.com.

First printing

1 3 5 7 9 8 6 4 2

Library of Congress Cataloging-in-Publication Data

Cashin, John
 Handguns : safety, selection, and use / John Cashin.
      pages cm. — (Responsible gun ownership)
 Audience: Grade 9 to 12.
 Includes bibliographical references and index.
    ISBN 978-1-61900-050-6 (hc)
    ISBN 978-1-61900-056-8 (trade)
    ISBN 978-1-61900-062-9 (ebook)
 1. Firearms. 2. Firearms—Safety measures. 3. Pistols.
 4. Pistols—Safety measures. I. Title.
 TS537.C37 2014
 683.4—dc23
                            2014000394

For information about custom editions, special sales, or premiums,
please contact our special sales department at info@eldoradoink.com.

Table of Contents

3

Chapter 1

Why Do You Want a Handgun?

Handguns are highly controversial. Some Americans believe that all guns are evil, and that they need to be tightly controlled by the government. Others argue that every American should own and carry a firearm for their own personal protection. The truth is that guns are neither inherently good nor inherently evil. A handgun is simply a tool. It can be used for good or bad purposes, depending on the owner's intent.

Many tools are dangerous when not used properly. A person who does not know how to safely handle a power saw or a snowblower risks serious injury. This is also true of guns. If a person is not properly prepared to handle and use a pistol or revolver, deadly accidents can happen. That's why it is essential for gun owners to be responsible. If you want to own a handgun, you must carefully choose the one that is right for you, and make sure you learn how to handle and use it safely.

If you are reading this book, chances are you are thinking about purchasing a handgun or want to know more about them. The purpose of this guide is to introduce prospective gun owners to many types of handguns and their uses. It will not tell you which gun to buy, but it should help you to make that decision for yourself, based on why you want a handgun. The book will also give you information about how to handle your gun safely and take care of it properly, and offer an overview of some of the ways you can enjoy a handgun.

WHAT IS A HANDGUN?

A handgun is a type of weapon meant to be fired while held in the shooter's hand or hands, with no other support. Firearms that have a stock so they can be supported against the user's shoulder, such as rifles and shotguns, are referred to as "long guns."

Many people use the terms *handgun* and *pistol* interchangeably. Technically, however, pistols are one of the two major types of handguns. A pistol has a single chamber that holds an ammunition cartridge (this is a brass shell that contains the bullet, plus the propellant and a primer). In a pistol, the chamber is part of the gun's barrel. The other type of handgun is the revolver, which has a single barrel but a revolving cylinder with five or six chambers holding cartridges. The cylinder rotates each time the weapon is fired, moving a loaded chamber into line with the barrel so that another shot can be fired.

The earliest handguns were invented in the 14th and 15th centuries. These weapons had single or double barrels that had to be reloaded each time a shot was fired. By the 16th century, firearms with revolving chambers holding the ammunition had been developed. However, these guns were awkward to use, as well as expensive and rare. As a result, the single-shot pistol remained the most common handgun until the mid-19th century.

HOW A REVOLVER WORKS

In 1836, an American inventor and gunsmith named Samuel Colt patented a design for a handgun with a revolving cylinder. This became the first practical revolver that was manufactured in the United States. It took several years for the new design to be widely accepted, but by the 1850s Colt revolvers were the most popular handguns in the United States and Europe.

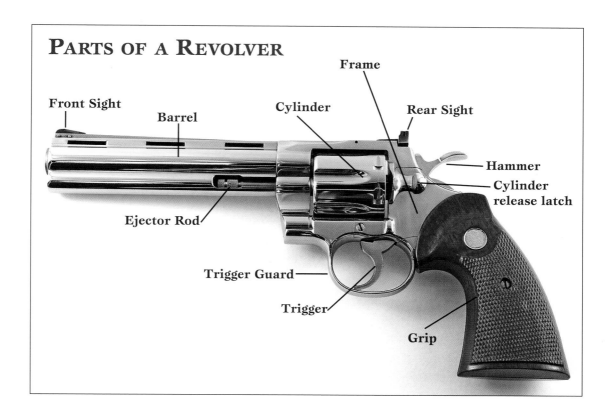

PARTS OF A REVOLVER

Front Sight

Barrel

Cylinder

Frame

Rear Sight

Hammer

Cylinder release latch

Ejector Rod

Trigger Guard

Trigger

Grip

Modern revolvers, which are based on Colt's design, have a cylinder that rotates into place when the gun is ready to be fired. The cylinder has a number of chambers, usually five or six, each of which holds an ammunition cartridge. Each time the gun is fired, the cylinder rotates so that the next chamber is aligned with the barrel. When the cylinder is empty, the shooter can release it so that it swings out on a hinge, called the crane. This way the chambers can be reloaded.

The mechanism that rotates the cylinder is known as the *action*. On the original Colt revolvers, the hammer had to be cocked, or pulled back into a firing position, before the gun could be fired. When the trigger is pulled, the cocked hammer is released and drops forward, striking the end of the cartridge where a priming device, called a percussion cap, is located. The percussion cap explodes, igniting the gunpowder in the cartridge and causing the bullet to be expelled through the barrel of the gun toward the target.

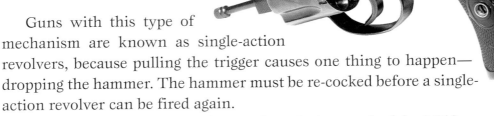

The cylinder of this revolver is open so that the handgun can be loaded.

Guns with this type of mechanism are known as single-action revolvers, because pulling the trigger causes one thing to happen—dropping the hammer. The hammer must be re-cocked before a single-action revolver can be fired again.

Samuel Colt's patent on the revolver design expired in 1856, so after that time other gunsmiths could freely incorporate his innovations into their own weapon designs. By the late 1880s, another American gun manufacturer, Smith & Wesson, had developed a more effective revolver action that eliminated the need for the shooter to manually cock the hammer. Pulling the trigger part of the way back would bring the hammer into a cocked position. Continuing to pull on the trigger would release the hammer and fire the weapon. Handguns with this type of mechanism became known as double-action revolvers. The double-action revolver is simpler to operate, because once it is loaded the shooter just has to aim and pull the trigger.

Single-action revolvers, like this .38 special, require the hammer to be pulled back (cocked) before the gun can be fired.

The main advantage of the double-action revolver over the single-action is that the shooter can cock and fire the gun without having to change the position of his or her hands between shots. One downside of the double action is that the shooter must exert greater force on the trigger in order to cock and fire the gun. To fire a double-action revolver with the hammer at rest against the frame takes about 12 pounds of pressure. To fire a single-action revolver with the hammer cocked takes 2 to 5 pounds of pressure. Consequently, many revolvers today are double/single-action, meaning they can be fired using either single action or double action. This allows the shooter to choose whether to manually cock his weapon before firing, or to pull the trigger through the entire sequence of cocking and firing.

THE SEMI-AUTOMATIC PISTOL

The development of the revolver revolutionized the firearms industry. The ability to fire five or six shots before reloading gave shooters much more firepower than a single-barreled pistol could provide.

As weapons technology improved, gunsmiths began to develop rifles and shotguns that could be fired multiple times before the user would need to stop and reload. The revolver mechanism was not suitable for long guns, because the open cylinder design allows the discharge of hot gases when the gun is fired. This is not a problem with a handgun that is held away from the body. However, when this action was tried on rifles the gas discharge was dangerously close to the shooter's face. So other innovations were created, such as placing an internal magazine—a device that can hold multiple ammunition cartridges—inside the rifle's stock or under the barrel. When a repeating rifle is fired the shooter works a mechanism, such as a bolt or lever, which ejects the spent shell and moves another one from the magazine into the chamber so it can be fired. By the end of the 19th century, gun designers had adapted the magazine and other concepts into pistol designs.

Modern pistols load cartridges into the barrel through a magazine that is typically placed inside the gun's handgrip. Most pistols today are semi-automatic, meaning that the user does not have to do any-

A semi-automatic pistol's magazine is typically loaded through the bottom of the handgrip. Most pistol magazines hold ammunition cartridges in a single column (or stack), as shown above. Each time the pistol is fired, a spring in the base of the magazine helps to push the ammunition cartridge at the top of the stack into the pistol's chamber.

thing but pull the trigger. Each time a semi-automatic handgun is fired, it immediately ejects the spent shell, loads a new one into the chamber, and resets the hammer. It is then ready to be fired again the next time the trigger is pulled, until the magazine is empty.

In most semi-automatic pistols, the way this works is that when a round is fired, some of the energy created by the exploding gunpowder in the cartridge is utilized to move a device called the *slide* to the rear of the handgun. This opens the chamber and ejects the spent shell casing. A spring mounted in the slide compresses as the slide moves backward. When the spring is fully compressed, the slide stops, and then moves forward. As it does this, the slide picks a round from the magazine and feeds it into the chamber, where it is ready to be fired the next time the trigger is pulled.

Just like revolvers, pistols are classified according to their action. There are single-action, double-action, and double/single-action pistols. There are also striker-fired pistols, which replace the traditional hammer action with a different mechanism that has fewer moving

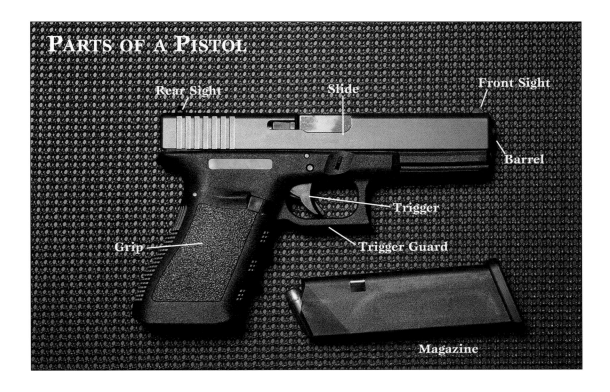

PARTS OF A PISTOL

Rear Sight

Slide

Front Sight

Barrel

Trigger

Grip

Trigger Guard

Magazine

parts. Developed by Austrian gunmaker Gaston Glock in the early 1980s, the striker-fired pistol has become the standard for law enforcement agents in the United States because of its light weight and ease of use.

UNDERSTANDING AMMUNITION

In addition to the two main types of handguns, and the various actions, handguns can also be separated into categories based on the size of the bullets they fire. The term *caliber* refers to the diameter of the inside of a gun barrel. This number is generally represented either as a fraction of an inch (such as .357 or .38) or as a metric figure (for example, 9 millimeters, or mm). The metric cartridges are sometimes listed with two numbers, with the second figure indicating the length of the cartridge. In most pistols used by law enforcement agents and soldiers, the 9x19mm cartridge (commonly called the Parabellum or NATO cartridge) is the standard ammunition.

The ammunition used in a handgun is properly called a cartridge, although it is sometimes referred to as a round. The cartridge consists of a brass case that holds a bullet, propellant (typically, smokeless powder), and an explosive primer. When the primer is struck forcefully, it explodes and ignites the propellant. This creates a great deal of pressure, expelling the bullet from the case and through the barrel toward its target.

There are two ways that the primer is placed in a handgun cartridge. Rimfire cartridges have the primer located inside the base of the cartridge. When this type of cartridge is struck sharply anywhere on the rim, the primer explodes. The brass casing of a rimfire cartridge is damaged when fired, so it can't be reloaded. Centerfire cartridges have the priming device set in the center of the cartridge base. Because the primer is a separate component, brass centerfire cases can be reloaded and reused. Today the most popular handgun cartridge sold in the United States is the .22 long rifle (LR) rimfire, which is used in sporting pistols. However, almost all higher-caliber ammunition sold today is centerfire.

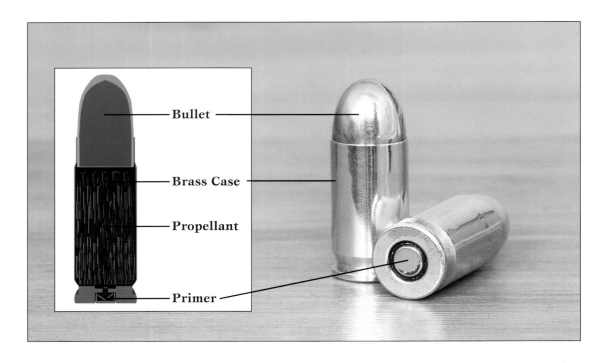

Some common handgun ammunition cartridges are (from left) the .22 LR rimfire, the most common cartridge sold in the United States; .22 Winchester Magnum, a more powerful small caliber cartridge; 9x19 mm Parabellum; .38 special flat point; .357 magnum semi-jacketed flat point; .44 magnum semi-jacketed flat point. Semi-jacketed, or soft point, bullets expand on impact to cause greater tissue damage, making them good for personal defense.

WHAT HANDGUN IS RIGHT FOR YOU?

The size and type of handgun you purchase will depend largely on what you intend to do with the gun. For example, a person who is interested in owning a gun for self-defense would not look to buy a hunting rifle or a small-caliber target pistol. There are four common reasons why a person wants to buy a gun: for personal defense, for sporting use such as target shooting, for hunting, and for collecting.

PERSONAL DEFENSE: Most American adults who purchase a handgun say that their primary reason is for personal defense. If someone tries to terrorize or harm you or your family, a firearm is a great equalizer—so long as you are prepared and have the will and skill to use the gun properly. Before purchasing a gun for self-defense, take time to carefully and honestly evaluate your personality and character. Do you know—not just think—that if some bad guy threatened you or your family, that you would be able to shoot him? If you're not sure that you'd be able to pull the trigger in that situation, you're probably better off not purchasing a gun. Criminals can sense fear and uncertainty, and if you hesitate, your gun might be taken away from you and used to prey on someone else. Instead, consider non-lethal alternatives for personal defense, such as pepper spray or martial arts training.

If you want to own a handgun for personal defense, you will need training in how to handle it properly, and you'll have to practice regularly.

If you intend to buy a handgun for personal defense, understand that you can't just purchase the weapon and keep it in a drawer by your bed until you need it. You have a responsibility to practice with the gun until you can use it well, and to keep it clean so that it works properly when you need it.

When you buy a gun for self-defense, you are looking for a weapon that fires bullets that will incapacitate the target, so that it no longer poses a threat to you. This is known as the bullet's "stopping power." High-powered ammunition cartridges—such as the .357 magnum, the .44 magnum, and the .45 auto—cause large wounds that in most cases will stop an attacker. However, the powerful recoil makes these hand-guns difficult to fire accurately, especially for a novice shooter. Handguns chambered for cartridges like 9 mm Parabellum, Smith &

Wesson .40, or .38 special are a little less powerful but can be just as effective.

Semi-automatic pistols and revolvers can both make effective self-defense weapons. There are advantages and drawbacks to each. Pistols have larger magazines—they can be fired 9 to 15 times before reloading, whereas the typical revolver can shoot five or six times. They also tend to have less recoil than revolvers. However, pistols have more complex action mechanisms, so they can be more likely to jam. A misfire will render a semi-automatic pistol inoperable until it is cleared. With a revolver, if one cartridge misfires the shooter simply has to pull the trigger again and the hammer will fall on the cartridge in the next chamber. Revolvers also are typically chambered for more powerful ammunition.

Many experts suggest that novice shooters choose a revolver as their first self-defense weapon. Once they have become more skilled with a handgun, a semi-automatic pistol may be a better choice. However, the bottom line is that if you're buying a gun for self-defense, you have to find the one that feels "right" in your hand.

HUNTING: When hunting is discussed, most people think of shotguns or high-powered rifles. However, there are plenty of people who enjoy the challenge of hunting deer and even larger game with handguns. And it is a challenge—hunting with a handgun is considerably more difficult than hunting with a rifle or shotgun. A handgun hunter must stalk his quarry to a much closer range, often 50 yards or less, and must place his shots perfectly to bring down the animal. Some animals hunted with handguns, such as wild boar or bears, can be very dangerous.

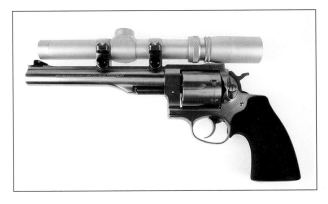

Powerful revolvers like this .44 magnum can be equipped with a scope and used for hunting.

For hunting, higher-caliber revolvers with long barrels are typically used. Often, these revolvers are chambered in .44, .45, or .50 caliber. There are also single-shot hunting handguns that are chambered for rifle cartridges, such as the .223, .270, .308, or .30-06. There are even highly specialized "hand cannons" with barrels that can be replaced, enabling the gun to fire a variety of ammunition depending on the prey.

Handguns used for hunting are generally equipped with a 2x scope—a telescopic sight that magnifies the target, making it appear twice as large as it actually is.

SPORTING USE: Many people simply want a gun because of the recreational benefits a firearm can provide. It can be very satisfying to be able to hit a target regularly, and fun to watch old cans dance or water bottles burst when hit with a bullet. *Plinking* is a name for

Target shooting can be a lot of fun, whether you are at a range or "plinking" informally in a safe outdoor area. Wherever you are shooting, it's important to always wear proper eye and ear protection.

Some people collect handguns, such as this 19th century Colt revolver. However, you should never fire any older gun without first having it examined by a competent gunsmith to make sure it is safe. Age and rust can weaken the chamber and barrel of older firearms, and some modern ammunition cartridges may be too powerful for antique weapons to fire safely.

informal target shooting, best done in rural areas. There are a variety of organized shooting sports available as well. More information on these is available in chapter 5.

Probably the most popular handgun for plinking and for many types of shooting sports is one that shoots the .22LR caliber. The ammunition is relatively inexpensive, and these types of guns are accurate. Because of the small caliber, there is little recoil, making them easier for novices to fire.

COLLECTING: People will collect anything—coins, stamps, baseball cards, and yes, firearms. Some people will collect guns from a certain period of history; others will try to find all models of a certain type of gun.

Chapter 2

Purchasing a Handgun

Once you know what you want to use a handgun for, you are ready for the next step—deciding which gun to buy. Understanding what you need a gun for will help to narrow down the choices. If you intend to carry your handgun for protection, you'll probably want something that is smaller and lighter than a handgun you would use for hunting. Don't purchase a gun because you think it looks cool, or because of its price. The proper handgun for you is one that suits your needs and that you can handle safely.

For most Americans, buying a firearm can be simple. You visit a local gun store or sporting goods store and choose the gun you want. You'll have to provide photo ID, fill out some forms, and pass a government-required background check before you can purchase a gun. However, some states have their own requirements for gun owners, which can make the process more cumbersome.

State and federal laws set the minimum age at which a person can purchase or own a handgun. You must be at least 21 years old in order to buy a handgun from a federally licensed firearms dealer. However, some states allow private sales of handguns to 18 year olds.

Before you're ready to buy, do some research on gun ownership in your state. As a starting point, the National Rifle Association maintains a state-by-state listing of gun laws related to firearms ownership online at http://www.nraila.org/gun-laws/state-laws.aspx. Another good source of information is the website www.handgunlaw.us, which contains information about state and federal statutes related to gun ownership.

VISITING THE GUN STORE

Before you purchase a gun, ask your friends who are gun owners for their opinion. Read articles about the merits and drawbacks of different types of guns. A gunsmith in your area, or the range master at a local shooting range, can also be a good source of information.

When you are ready to buy, the clerk in your local gun store should be able to help you find the best gun for you. If you're a first-time buyer, let the clerk know. It's his job to sell you the right firearm for your needs. Most gun store clerks are knowledgeable and will take the time to show you various handguns and explain their advantages and disadvantages, if you'll let them. If at any time you feel like you are being rushed, or pressured to purchase something that doesn't feel right to you, you can always leave the store and try someplace else.

Typically, when you ask the salesperson to see a specific gun, he will take the weapon from the display case, point it in a safe direction, and open the action to make sure that the gun is not loaded. Then he will hand you the gun. The first thing you should do once you take the gun is to check for yourself to make sure it is not loaded. This means opening the action to make sure there is not a round of ammunition in the chamber. Once you've ascertained for yourself that the weapon is not loaded, you can safely examine it.

As you're looking over the handgun, remember this important point of etiquette: never point a gun at the clerk or any other person in the store. No one is comfortable having a gun pointed at him or her. It's a good safety practice to always treat every gun as if it is loaded, even when you know it's not, and never point a gun at anything you don't intend to shoot.

A federally licensed gun dealer should be able to answer your questions and help you find the best handgun for your needs.

The way the gun feels in your hand is important. Some people have smaller hands, so a high-caliber handgun may feel large and awkward to them. Others with larger hands may find it hard to grip a compact "pocket pistol" properly. You want a handgun that fits your body well. A gun store salesperson may allow you to hold two different handguns simultaneously, so you can compare the way they feel. Some stores will only let you handle one gun at a time.

Pulling the trigger on an unloaded gun lets you test the action and get a sense of how much force is needed to fire. Because there is no cartridge in the chamber, this is known as "dry-firing." However, dry-firing can damage some guns, particularly those that use rimfire cartridges. Before you dry-fire a handgun, make sure to ask the salesperson if it's OK. If you get permission, don't snap away a dozen times. You'll only need to pull the trigger once or twice to get a feel for the gun's action.

GUN SHOWS

Gun stores are not the only place where you can look at, and handle, different types of handguns. If you want to see a lot of guns in a short period of time, attend a local gun show. A variety of vendors rent tables at these events to promote and sell their products, which may include not only guns, but also ammunition, gun accessories, books, hunting and camping equipment, and other items related to shooting sports. Typically, there is a door charge to enter the show, and you'll be asked to go through a security checkpoint before you enter.

You will typically find two types of vendors at a gun show. Most vendors—approximately 50 to 75 percent, according to a study by the

Before attending a gun show, do some research so you are familiar with the retail price of handguns that you're interested in buying. If you know what a gun would cost in a store, you may be able to negotiate a lower price with a dealer at a show. Also, you'll probably get a better price if you're willing to pay cash at the show.

Bureau of Alcohol, Tobacco, and Firearms—are federally licensed dealers. They are usually the owners of gun stores who bring inventory to sell during the show. These dealers have a license from the federal government that allows them to sell firearms. When selling a gun, they are required to follow all federal, state, and local laws regarding paperwork, background checks, and the like. However, some vendors are simply individuals who rent a table at the sale intending to sell guns that they own. In most states, these private individuals are not required to fill out federal paperwork or perform background checks because it is legal for them to sell a firearm to another person.

At the present time, 18 of the 50 U.S. states regulate private firearm sales at gun shows. Seven states—California, Colorado, Connecticut, Illinois, New York, Oregon, and Rhode Island—require background checks on all firearm sales at gun shows. Five other states—Florida, Hawaii, Maryland, New Jersey, and Pennsylvania—require background checks on all handgun purchases at gun shows. In these states, long guns can be sold privately without background checks. Seven states—Iowa, Florida, Massachusetts, Michigan, Minnesota, Nebraska, and North Carolina—require individuals to obtain a permit before they can purchase handguns at a gun show; the permit application process includes a background check. The other states do not restrict private sales of firearms at gun shows.

When exploring a gun show, the same rules for examining the handgun apply. Always point the gun in a safe direction, never at another person. Gun shows are often crowded, so be respectful of safety rules and considerate of the vendors' time. Also, keep in mind that there are disadvantages to buying at a gun show. You won't be able to test-fire the gun before you purchase it, for example, and generally there are no warranties for handguns sold by private individuals.

TRY BEFORE YOU BUY

When shopping for a handgun, don't feel that you have to purchase one right away. After you've seen several different models and have an idea of what you like, it's a good idea to test-fire the guns before making a decision. One way to do this is to go to a local shooting range and ask about renting the handgun model that you like, so you can fire it at the range. This is a great way to try different handguns and determine which model you like best.

You'll usually be asked to fill out a waiver form when you rent a handgun at a firing range. You may also be required to purchase ammunition and targets at the range. Once everything is in order, the range master will explain the rules and assign you a shooting position. In most indoor firing ranges, shooters fire handguns at a target hung at the end of a lane. A pulley system enables the shooter to adjust the distance to the target; usually, the target can be as close as 15 feet or as far as 100 feet away. For a novice shooter, 15 to 25 feet is a good starting point. There often are concrete partitions separating the shooters in adjacent lanes for safety.

Some ranges will allow you to turn in the first handgun and rent a second handgun. This allows you to compare how each model fires, and determine which one feels better in your hand. Sometimes, a firing range will have a store attached, so you can purchase the gun right there once you've tried it. Otherwise, you will have to go to a separate gun store once you've decided to purchase a particular model.

PAPERWORK AND BACKGROUND CHECKS

When you decide to buy a handgun from a federally licensed dealer,

U.S. Department of Justice
Bureau of Alcohol, Tobacco, Firearms and Explosives

OMB No. 1140-0020

**Firearms Transaction Record Part I -
Over-the-Counter**

WARNING: You may not receive a firearm if prohibited by Federal or State law. The information you provide will be used to determine whether you are prohibited under law from receiving a firearm. Certain violations of the Gun Control Act, 18 U.S.C. §§ 921 et. seq., are punishable by up to 10 years imprisonment and/or up to a $250,000 fine.

Transferor's Transaction Serial Number (If any)

Prepare in original only. All entries must be handwritten in ink. Read the Notices, Instructions, and Definitions on this form. "PLEASE PRINT."

Section A - Must Be Completed Personally By Transferee (Buyer)

1. Transferee's Full Name
Last Name / First Name / Middle Name (If no middle name, state "NMN")

2. Current Residence Address (U.S. Postal abbreviations are acceptable. Cannot be a post office box.)
Number and Street Address / City / County / State / ZIP Code

3. Place of Birth
U.S. City and State -OR- Foreign Country
4. Height (Ft. / In.)
5. Weight (Lbs.)
6. Gender: Male / Female
7. Birth Date: Month / Day / Year

8. Social Security Number (Optional, but will help prevent misidentification)
9. Unique Personal Identification Number (UPIN) if applicable (See Instructions for Question 9.)

10.a. Ethnicity
Hispanic or Latino / Not Hispanic or Latino

10.b. Race (Check one or more boxes.)
American Indian or Alaska Native / Asian / Black or African American / Native Hawaiian or Other Pacific Islander / White

11. Answer questions 11.a. (see exceptions) through 11.l. and 12 (if applicable) by checking or marking "yes" or "no" in the boxes to the right of the questions.

a. Are you the actual transferee/buyer of the firearm(s) listed on this form? Warning: You are not the actual buyer if you are acquiring the firearm(s) on behalf of another person. If you are not the actual buyer, the dealer cannot transfer the firearm(s) to you. (See Instructions for Question 11.a.) Exception: If you are picking up a repaired firearm(s) for another person, you are not required to answer 11.a. and may proceed to question 11.b. — Yes / No

b. Are you under indictment or information in any court for a felony, or any other crime, for which the judge could imprison you for more than one year? (See Instructions for Question 11.b.) — Yes / No

c. Have you ever been convicted in any court of a felony, or any other crime, for which the judge could have imprisoned you for more than one year, even if you received a shorter sentence including probation? (See Instructions for Question 11.c.) — Yes / No

d. Are you a fugitive from justice? — Yes / No

e. Are you an unlawful user of, or addicted to, marijuana or any depressant, stimulant, narcotic drug, or any other controlled substance? — Yes / No

f. Have you ever been adjudicated mentally defective (which includes a determination by a court, board, commission, or other lawful authority that you are a danger to yourself or to others or are incompetent to manage your own affairs) OR have you ever been committed to a mental institution? (See Instructions for Question 11.f.) — Yes / No

g. Have you been discharged from the Armed Forces under dishonorable conditions? — Yes / No

h. Are you subject to a court order restraining you from harassing, stalking, or threatening your child or an intimate partner or child of such partner? (See Instructions for Question 11.h.) — Yes / No

A firearms transaction record, or form 4473, must be filled out when you purchase a handgun from a federally licensed dealer.

you'll have to complete some paperwork. The dealer will ask you to fill out a "firearms transaction record," or Form 4473. You'll be required to answer many personal questions. You'll also record the serial number and other information about the firearm you are buying, and you'll affirm that you are not prohibited from purchasing a gun. Along with Form 4473, you'll submit a copy of your driver's license (or another state-issued photo ID).

The dealer must keep this form on file in a log book for 20 years, and is required to turn over the logbook for inspection by federal authorities if they ever request it as part of a criminal investigation.

Once form 4473 is filled out, the dealer will access the National Instant Criminal Background Check System. This is a federal database, administered by the FBI, which determines whether a person is legally permitted to purchase a firearm. A federal law called the Gun Control Act of 1968 prohibits certain people from owning firearms. You can't buy a gun if you've been sentenced to prison for more than a year, have been convicted of a violent crime, or have been diagnosed as mentally ill. Sometimes the background check can be completed in a matter of minutes. In other cases, it can take up to three days before the dealer is permitted to complete the sale. So when you go to purchase a handgun, be prepared to leave the store without it in case the background check takes hours or days to complete.

Chapter 3

Rules of Gun Safety

Once you've bought a gun, the very first thing you need to do is learn how to use it properly and handle it safely. Read the owner's manual carefully, so that you thoroughly understand how your handgun works. You would do this with any complex and potentially dangerous tool, such as an automobile or a power saw. Keep your unloaded gun nearby while you're reading the manual, so that you can look at illustrations and work the safety catch and action so that you're familiar with how the gun operates. If you own a semi-automatic pistol, it's particularly important to understand how to unload it safely and how to clear jams.

10 COMMANDMENTS OF GUN SAFETY

Most handgun accidents happen because a person did not follow proper safety procedures. To reduce accidents, over the years a set of guidelines for the safe handling and use of firearms have been developed. Novice gun owners should familiarize themselves with these "10 commandments of gun

Always assume that a gun is loaded, even if you were the last person to use it. Before handling any firearm, visually inspect the chamber and magazine to make sure they do not contain ammunition. Don't take anyone else's word for this—always check for yourself.

safety" before they handle a handgun. As a general principle, you should treat every handgun as though it is loaded—even when you are certain that the gun is not loaded.

1. ALWAYS POINT THE GUN BARREL IN A SAFE DIRECTION. A safe direction is one in which an accidental discharge will not cause injury to yourself or to another person. You should never point a gun at another person, unless you intend to shoot that person in self-defense. Even if your handgun is unloaded, be aware of the direction it is pointed. This rule is particularly important to observe when you are loading or unloading the weapon.

2. KEEP YOUR HANDGUN UNLOADED WHEN YOU ARE NOT USING IT. Your gun should only be loaded when you are on a target range or in the field ready to fire. When you are finished shooting, unload the firearm completely—this means making sure there is no ammunition in the chamber(s) or in the magazine. Never let a loaded gun out of your sight.

3. DON'T RELY ON YOUR GUN'S SAFETY. All semi-automatic pistols have a safety catch, which when engaged will keep the gun from firing. However, the safety does not excuse anyone from following safe gun handling procedures. Like any mechanical device, the safety could fail, or a novice gun owner might think the safety is on when it is not. Treat your gun as though it could fire at any time, and even when the safety is engaged keep the handgun pointed in a safe direction. Get in the habit of keeping your index finger outside the gun's trigger guard. Never place your finger on the trigger until you are ready to fire.

4. BE SURE OF YOUR TARGET AND WHAT IS BEHIND IT. Bullets can travel long distances, and can ricochet off stones and other hard surfaces, or even water. Before you fire, be aware of what might happen if you miss. Be aware, also, of the penetrating power of the ammunition you are shooting. Full metal jacketed bullets may go through even a solid target and hit something on the other side. The same is true of large-caliber bullets fired with magnum propellant loads. If possible, any time you are shooting outdoors make sure there is some sort of backstop behind your target. Ideally, this would be a hillside or berm made of dense material like sand or dirt.

5. ALWAYS USE THE PROPER AMMUNITION FOR YOUR HANDGUN. Every gun is designed to use a certain caliber of ammunition. Using the wrong ammunition can destroy your firearm and seriously injure you. Refer to the owner's manual for your gun to determine exactly what size ammunition you should be using, as well as the maximum propellant load your gun can handle. Always check your ammunition carefully before loading it into your weapon.

As a general rule, it's a good idea to carry only one caliber of ammunition when you are shooting. This may help prevent you from accidentally loading the wrong size cartridges in your handgun.

6. IF YOUR HANDGUN FAILS TO FIRE WHEN THE TRIGGER IS PULLED, HANDLE WITH CARE. Stop and remember the First Commandment—keep the muzzle pointed in a safe direction. Never try to look down the barrel or put your face close to the *breech*. Engage the safety (if your gun has one), then follow the steps outlined in the owner's manual for how to clear a misfire or jam. This typically involves opening the action and unloading the firearm. Dispose of the bad cartridge safely.

7. ALWAYS WEAR EYE AND EAR PROTECTION WHEN SHOOT-ING. Your hearing and sight can be permanently damaged when shooting. Specific information on ear and eye protection is available on pages 30–32 of this chapter.

8. BE SURE THE BARREL IS CLEAR OF OBSTRUCTIONS BEFORE SHOOTING. Before you load your gun, open the action and make sure there is nothing in the chamber or magazine. Look through the bore to make sure there is no obstruction. Even a small amount of dirt or excess grease inside the barrel can cause a dangerous spike in pressure that can damage your gun. If the gun barrel bursts, it's likely you'll be seriously injured. If you see something, clean and lubricate your unloaded gun properly before you fire it.

9. HAVE YOUR GUN SERVICED REGULARLY. Like any mechanical device, a handgun requires regular maintenance to remain in good working condition. You can do some of this maintenance, such as routine cleaning, yourself. (The general cleaning procedure is discussed on pages 36–39 of this book.) For complex maintenance or repairs, find a competent gunsmith. Depending on where you live, a federally licensed gunsmith may charge $50 to $75 an hour, plus the cost of parts or materials, for repairs. The owner's manual should have a schedule for period inspection and adjustment by the gunsmith.

Never alter or modify your handgun. It was designed by experts to function properly in its original condition. Any modifications to the trigger, safety, or other parts can make the gun dangerous to operate, and will almost certainly void any warranty provided by the manufacturer.

10. LEARN THE CHARACTERISTICS OF THE HANDGUN YOU ARE USING. Not all guns are alike; they all have different mechanical and handling characteristics. Make sure that you are totally familiar with how to safely load, handle, unload, carry, shoot, and store your handgun. Do not use any firearm that you have not had adequate instruction in handling.

Firing a handgun with a dirty barrel is dangerous. Make sure to clean your gun every time you use it, and have it occasionally checked by a reputable gunsmith.

According to recent data, there are about 30,000 firearm-related deaths in the United States each year. About 30 percent of these deaths also involve alcohol.

ALWAYS SHOOT SOBER

Another critical safety rule is never to use drugs or drink alcohol when handling firearms. Drugs and alcohol affect a person's brain and central nervous system. A person who is under the influence of drugs or alcohol can become more easily angered or upset, while also losing control of the fine motor skills needed to safely use a gun. Drugs and alcohol also reduce a person's inhibitions, making him or her more likely to take dangerous risks. All these things make alcohol, drugs, and guns a deadly combination.

Most of the shooting accidents that occur each year involve alcohol or drug use. So be smart and never consume anything that might impair your judgment or physical coordination when you plan to use your handgun.

EYE AND EAR PROTECTION

As the Seventh Commandment notes, every handgun owner must use safety glasses and ear protection when shooting.

Shooting safety glasses are relatively inexpensive. They will protect your eyes from any small, hot pieces of lead or brass shell casings that might come flying your way while shooting, as well as from dust, muzzle flashes, and gunpowder residue. Regular eyeglasses do offer some protection from the front, but generally the sides are not protected. This area is at the greatest risk of being hit by a hot shell casing ejected from the gun of a shooter standing next to you at the range. A person who wears corrective lenses can order prescription safety glasses for shooting, which will provide protection for the front and sides. Generally, firing ranges require people to wear safety glasses when shooting.

Most firing ranges, especially indoor ones, also require shooters to wear ear protection. A gunshot can reach decibel (dB) levels over 150dB—well above the sound level that is painful for humans (about 120dB), and uncomfortably close to the decibel level where a person's eardrum can instantly burst (160dB). Prolonged exposure to noise above 85dB can cause permanent hearing loss. Therefore, any time you are shooting, ear protection is a necessity. The two most common types of ear protection are ear muffs and earplugs.

There are numerous types of earplugs available. Single use earplugs are inexpensive foam plugs that can be discarded after they've been used. This is probably the most common type of ear protection. Multiple use earplugs are a little higher quality and, as the name implies, these can be washed and reused numerous times. Banded earplugs are mount-

Any time you shoot, proper eye and ear protection are essential.

ed on a plastic headband. This is convenient if you will be going into and out of a loud area like a firing range, as you can easily put them in and take them out without losing the earplugs.

A more expensive, but also more effective, option is molded silicone earplugs. Generally, a company will manufacture these using impressions taken from the insides of your ears. They can be expensive—often costing more than $100—and may take several weeks before you receive them. However, because they are specifically fitted to your ear, they reduce noise better than the generic foam earplugs. Molded earplugs will generally last for several years and require little care.

In recent years, many inexpensive do-it-yourself kits for making molded earplugs have become available. While these kits are cheaper and enable you to get your earplugs faster, they do have some drawbacks. The earplugs are usually made from a lower-quality material, and they may not fit your ear as well as the professional lab-made versions.

There are two types of earmuffs: electronic or passive. Electronic earmuffs are equipped with microphones and electronic circuits, which enable them to amplify quieter sounds while dampening loud sounds. This allows a shooter to hear the range master's commands clearly while simultaneously protecting his hearing from high decibel shooting sounds. Passive earmuffs simply block sound using foam and other materials located inside the ear cup.

Whatever type of ear protection you choose, make sure to check the product's Noise Reduction Rating (NRR). This number indicates the maximum number of decibels that the hearing protector will reduce the sound level when worn. The highest NRR rating you can get is 33. For indoor shooting, you should get products with an NRR of 28 or higher.

Chapter 4

Caring for Your Handgun

A ll gun owners are responsible for keeping their firearm out of unauthorized hands. To date, 18 U.S. states have passed child access prevention (CAP) laws. These are intended to prevent firearm injuries by limiting children's access to guns. The CAP laws establish criminal penalties for gun owners who do not properly store their guns. Under some CAP laws, it is a felony offense if an injury results from a child accessing an unsecured gun.

Consider buying a gun cabinet or gun safe to store your handgun. Look for a gun cabinet that is made out of stamped steel and has a sturdy lock. Cabinets made of wood and glass may look nice, but they won't stop someone who really wants to get their hands on your gun. Smaller steel gun cabinets often have pre-drilled holes so they can be bolted to the wall. This prevents someone from carting off the entire cabinet and opening it at their leisure.

Unlike cabinets, gun safes are generally fireproof and waterproof, so they provide more protection for your guns. Gun safes are heavier and have sturdier locks, so they are also more expensive. Companies

A cable lock (left) renders a handgun unusable by making it impossible to load a cartridge into the breech or a magazine into the grip.

Trigger locks (below) prevent access to the firearm's trigger. Some can be unlocked with a key; others are combination locks.

like Liberty, Browning, and Fort Knox are respected manufacturers of quality gun safes. It's a good idea to purchase a gun safe that is larger than you need—many people's gun collections will grow over time, and a gun safe can be used to store other valuables as well.

Many people prefer to keep a large gun safe in an out-of-the-way place, such as a basement or utility room. This is not ideal for a person who purchased a handgun with personal protection in mind. Smaller gun safes are available that can be mounted to the headboard of a bed, or to a nightstand or other piece of bedroom furniture. These safes, made by companies like Titan Security or GunVault, hold a single pistol or revolver. They typically have a touch keypad that can be manipulated in darkness to open the safe and allow quick access to the gun.

There are also various types of devices that are used to prevent guns from being fired by anyone not authorized by the gun owner. Some gun manufacturers, including Smith & Wesson, Taurus, and Ruger, provide an internal trigger locking mechanism on their firearms. These mechanisms lock the action so that the gun cannot be fired unless they are unlocked with a key.

Trigger locks are also available for other handguns. These usually consist of two pieces that, when locked together, surround the trigger guard and make it physically impossible to pull the trigger. These trigger locks can usually be unlocked with a key or a combination.

There are two downsides to this sort of trigger lock. One is that they do not necessarily prevent a loaded weapon from being fired. Certain types of handguns can go off if they are dropped. The other downside is the time it can take to undo a trigger lock. A gun owner faced with a self-defense situation will not want to have to fumble with a key or combination in order to make his handgun ready.

Another type of safety device, the chamber lock, makes it impossible to load ammunition into a handgun's chamber. This prevents the gun from being fired. Cable locks are a popular type of chamber lock. The cable threads through the breech, so a cartridge cannot be loaded. It also runs through the grip of a semi-automatic pistol, so that a magazine cannot be loaded properly.

Someone who is determined to get at your guns can bypass any type of safe or gun lock. To help make your home safer, children under the age of 10 must be instructed never to handle a handgun.

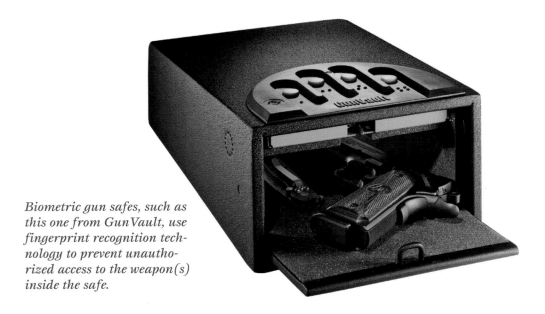

Biometric gun safes, such as this one from GunVault, use fingerprint recognition technology to prevent unauthorized access to the weapon(s) inside the safe.

Some people say ammunition should be stored in a separate place from firearms, so that an unauthorized person cannot access both at the same time. Others feel it is OK to lock ammunition inside of a gun safe with their handgun. Either way, ammunition should always be stored in a cool, dry place.

The NRA has a program for children between the ages of 5 and 10 called Eddie Eagle. It advocates teaching a four-step safety procedure for children who find a gun: stop, don't touch, leave the area, and tell an adult. Information about the program is available online at http://eddieeagle.nra.org.

Cleaning Your Handgun

Shooting your gun is a dirty business. Each time a handgun is fired, the propellant leaves burnt powder residue in the action, chamber, and barrel. As the bullet travels through the gun barrel, it deposits small amounts of copper or lead inside the rifled grooves in the barrel. If the rifling is not cleaned of the powder residue and bullet fragments, your handgun's accuracy will be impaired. A dirty handgun can even be unsafe to fire. You should clean a gun after every time you fire it. This is especially true after target practice, when you may have fired dozens or hundreds of rounds.

Most gun stores and sporting goods stores will sell a basic gun cleaning kit. These kits contains just about everything a novice gun owner will need to get started. The kit should have a rod and rod accessories, along with gun oil, cloth patches, and a bottle of solvent that dissolves caked-on powder. You may also need to buy a wire bore brush that fits your firearm, as well as a package of cotton bore patches of the appropriate diameter.

To clean your handgun, find an area that is free of clutter and is large enough to place all your tools and the parts of your gun where they can easily be accessed. You'll want to do your cleaning in a place with good lighting, as springs and small pieces can easily fall and get lost. Also, make sure you give yourself plenty of time to complete the job. You don't want to rush, as you might reassemble your firearm incorrectly and that will cause trouble the next time you want to shoot. It's also a good idea to wear protective glasses and rubber gloves when cleaning a gun. Small droplets of solvent can splash into your eye or irritate your skin.

The first step in cleaning is to make sure that the gun is unloaded. If you have a semi-automatic pistol, remove the magazine and make sure there is no cartridge in the chamber. Once this is done, consult the owner's manual and follow the instructions to disassemble your handgun so it can be cleaned. For a revolver, this usually

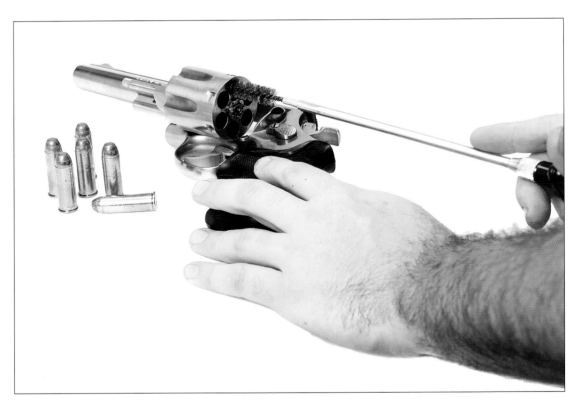

When cleaning a handgun, don't dip the bore brush directly into the solvent bottle, as this will foul the solvent. Instead, hold the brush over a clean container and pour solvent onto it. The left-over solvent in the container can be used to soak patches.

entails removing the cylinder. For a semi-automatic pistol, you'll probably have to remove the slide from the frame, and the barrel and recoil spring/guide from the slide. Wipe all of these pieces down with a clean, dry cloth.

Next, apply some solvent to the wire bore brush and push it back and forth through the barrel several times. You may have to clean the brush and reapply solvent once or twice. You should do this until the barrel has been thoroughly scrubbed. Then, soak a gun-cleaning patch in solvent and use the rod to push it through the barrel until it comes out the other end (don't bring it back through). The first patch will come out dirty; you'll have to repeat this four or five times, until the patch comes through clean.

This process is done once on a semi-automatic pistol. If you own a revolver, you'll have to brush and swab not only the barrel, but also each chamber in the cylinder as well.

Next, use a soft bristle brush dipped in solvent to clean any surface that may be fouled. This includes the outside of a revolver's cylinder and ratchet, the inside of a pistol's slide, the contact points between the slide and the frame, and the outside of the barrel. Be thorough—if something looks dirty, clean it. Once you're finished, wipe off excess solvent with a dry lint-free cloth.

Handguns have mechanical parts that require proper lubrication. The actual areas that require lubrication with the gun oil will vary depending on the type of handgun. In general, the moving parts of a semi-automatic pistol's action all need to be oiled. Revolvers need less lubrication. Single-action revolvers will need some oil on the cylinder pin and ratchet, while double-action revolvers will also need oil on the ejector rod. Be careful not to use too much oil, as this will attract dust and dirt, causing the gun to become fouled more quickly.

Next, run a patch that is lightly lubricated with oil down the barrel, as well as down each chamber of a revolver.

Once this is done, follow the manufacturer's instructions to reassemble the firearm. If any excess oil oozes out of joints, wipe it off with a dry cloth. Always store your gun in a clean, dry place.

Chapter 5

Shooting Your Handgun

If you are a novice gun owner, it's a good idea to take a course in shooting from a licensed instructor. Shooting instructors understand what they are doing, and more importantly, know how to teach you to shoot and handle your firearm properly. Learning how to do things correctly will make you an accurate, fundamentally sound shooter.

You can find courses in your area that are taught by certified National Rifle Association instructors through the NRA's website, http://www.nrainstructors.org/searchcourse.aspx. This allows you to choose the course that you want to take, and search by zip code to find a qualified instructor in your area.

HOLDING A HANDGUN PROPERLY

Any time you pick up a handgun, remember the first safety commandment—the barrel must be pointed in a safe direction. This can't be stressed enough.

Start by placing the handgun grip in the webbing between your index finger and thumb of your dominant hand. Your thumb should wrap around one side of the grip, while the middle, ring, and pinky fingers are curled securely around the other side, just below the trigger guard. Your index finger will be used to pull the trigger; it should be kept outside the trigger guard until you are ready to fire your weapon.

Grip the gun as tightly as you can using your middle and ring fingers. This will help to control the gun's recoil. A gun that is not held tightly will kick and jump when fired, reducing the accuracy of your subsequent shots.

Use your non-dominant hand to steady the handgun. When the weapon is held in two hands, both thumbs should point downrange at the target. When firing a semi-automatic pistol, place your hands so that your thumbs won't be struck when the slide moves backward. If you're not paying attention, you'll suffer a painful injury.

THE PROPER SHOOTING STANCE

A good stance provides a strong, stable platform, which is crucial for accurate shooting. The two most commonly used upright stances for shooting a handgun are the Isosceles Stance and the Weaver Stance. There are many other handgun shooting stances, but most are variations of one of these two stances.

The Isosceles Stance is a two-handed shooting stance often taught to beginners because it is effective yet simple and easy to remember under stress. It allows the shooter to cover a wide area simply by rotating his or her upper torso from side to side. When using the Isosceles Stance, you'll face the target with your feet shoulder-width apart and your knees slightly bent. Your shoulders should be square to the target. Holding the gun in both hands, you will raise your arms, keeping them straight and locked, until they are fully extended toward the target. When this is done properly, the arms form an isosceles triangle. The handgun should be raised to eye level, so that you can use the gunsights to aim.

A Los Angeles law enforcement agent named Jack Weaver developed the Weaver Stance in the 1950s, and it quickly became popular among police and military shooters because it allows accuracy while presenting a smaller profile. The Weaver Stance will probably look

The Isosceles Stance is easy for beginning shooters to master and is appropriate for personal defense.

familiar, as it is the shooting stance often used by policemen in movies and television shows.

In this two-handed stance, the dominant hand holds the handgun at eye level while the other hand wraps around it for support. Your elbows should be bent, with the support elbow pointing straight down. You'll stand with feet shoulder-width apart. However, unlike the Isosceles Stance your feet will not be square to the target. Instead, the dominant-side foot (for a right-handed shooter, this would be the right foot) should be set slightly behind the other in what looks like a boxer's stance. The toes of your rear foot should point out at about a 45 degree angle. Then you'll bend your knees and lean forward slightly, putting most of your weight on the forward foot.

There are several variations of each of these common stances. For example, a version known as the Modified Weaver requires the shooter to fully extend and lock his shooting arm, rather than leaving the elbow bent. It is believed

The Weaver Stance is a stable shooting position that provides good accuracy.

Soldiers and law enforcement officials are often trained to use the Modified Weaver Stance, in which the shooting arm is locked while the support arm's elbow points down.

that this reduces movement and improves accuracy. Ultimately, it's a good idea for a novice shooter to learn several different stances, and practice shooting with each of them, so he can choose the one that feels most comfortable and has the best results.

AIMING AND FIRING

Once you are in your stance, raise your weapon to eye level. This is done so that you can align the front and rear sights and aim your handgun properly.

All people have a "dominant eye"—one eye that is stronger and can focus more accurately than the other. Aiming with the dominant eye will make you a better shooter, so it's important to figure out which is the dominant eye. For most people, the dominant eye is on the same side as the dominant hand. For example, a left-handed person is likely to be left-eye dominant. However, some people are cross-dominant—they may be right-handed but left-eye dominant, for example. To determine your dominant eye, point your finger at a distant object with both eyes open. If you close your left eye and your finger remains pointed at the distant object, you are right-eye dominant.

For beginners, it is generally best to aim using only the dominant eye, with the other eye closed. The front sight should be aimed just below the point where you want the bullet to go. For example, when you are target shooting align the front sight with the bottom edge of the black bullseye. Make sure that the top of the front sight is level with the top of the rear sight, and that the front post is centered within the notch on the rear sight, as shown below.

Once your weapon has been brought to bear, place your finger inside the trigger guard and slowly squeeze the trigger. A consistent pull on the trigger will be more accurate than a sudden jerk, which can disrupt your aim. Good shooters time their shots with their breathing. They will take a breath, exhale, and then squeeze the trigger. After the gun goes off, continue to pull the trigger through until it stops, then release it and prepare for the next shot.

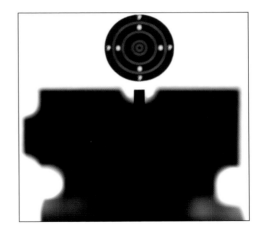

Each time a handgun is fired, the recoil from the shot will move your handgun off its original line to the target. Take time to re-aim your gun before firing again.

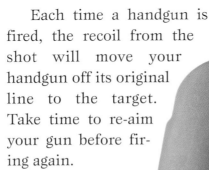

TIPS FOR SHOOTING PRACTICE

Like any sport, the more you practice the more accurate a shooter you will become. But shooting practice has to be effective. Take your time between shots, so that you can make certain that your stance and aiming techniques are fundamentally sound. Firing a group of shots quickly will make a lot of noise, but won't do much to make you a more accurate shooter.

Remember the key rules of firearm safety—always assume that your handgun is loaded, and only point it in a safe direction. Often, when beginners are re-loading their handguns they will point them to the side instead of downrange. This is particularly common among beginners using automatic pistols, as they may have a hard time pulling back, or "racking," the slide to eject a round or clear a jam. The best technique, however, is for you to turn your body sideways before trying to rack the slide. This way, the gun will always remain pointed in a safe direction downrange.

CARRYING A CONCEALED HANDGUN IN PUBLIC

The most common reason people say that they buy a handgun is for personal defense. Some people will be content to keep their gun at home, where it can be easily accessed in case someone tries to break in. Others, however, may wish to carry their gun with them when they are out in public. To do this, you must be careful to obey the laws related to carrying a concealed weapon, which vary from state to state. Failure to observe state and local laws regarding carrying or transporting firearms will result in stiff penalties, often including prison time.

As of 2014, every state allows its citizens to apply for a permit to carry a concealed weapon (CCW). However, the ease or difficulty of actually getting a CCW permit can vary greatly from state to state. In this respect, states can be divided into three categories. *Unrestricted jurisdictions* allow residents to carry a handgun without requiring them to apply for a permit. Today five states—Alaska, Arizona, Arkansas, Vermont, and Wyoming—are unrestricted jurisdictions.

Shall-issue states are those that must issue a CCW permit to anyone who meets the criteria for the permit. The criteria may include a minimum age, proof of residency in the state, passage of a background check, and/or completion of a firearm safety class. The following 37 states are considered shall-issue: Alabama, Colorado, Florida, Georgia, Idaho, Illinois, Indiana, Iowa, Kansas, Kentucky, Louisiana, Maine, Michigan, Minnesota, Mississippi, Missouri, Montana, Nebraska, Nevada, New Hampshire, New Mexico, North Carolina, North Dakota, Ohio, Oklahoma, Oregon, Pennsylvania, Rhode Island, South Carolina, South Dakota, Tennessee, Texas, Utah, Virginia, Washington, West Virginia, and Wisconsin.

May-issue states also require CCW permit applicants to fulfill certain criteria. However, in these jurisdictions local or state law enforcement officials have discretion to decide whether or not to issue the permit. These states typically require gun owners to show "good cause" before they will grant a CCW permit. As a result, it is much

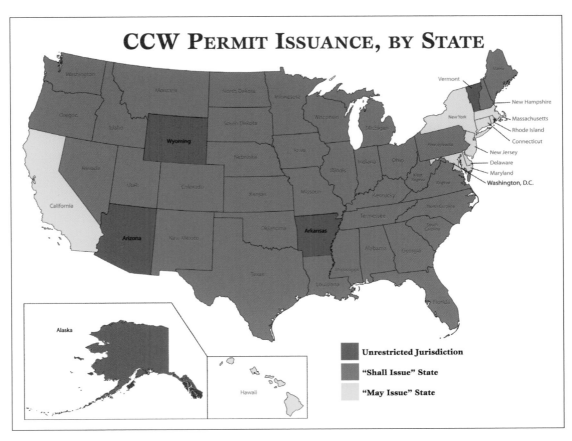

If you are traveling outside of your home state, you will have to respect the laws of every state that you pass through with regard to the transportation of firearms. This is true even if you're just driving through on an interstate highway. In general, you should have no trouble if your firearm is unloaded, is inside a locked case, and is stowed in the vehicle's trunk or some other area that is not immediately accessible. Ammunition should be stored in a separate locked container. The National Rifle Association provides a useful guide on this issue at http://www.nraila.org/gun-laws/articles/2010/guide-to-the-interstate-transportation.aspx

more difficult for residents of may-issue states to carry concealed handguns. May-issue states include California, Connecticut, Delaware, Hawaii, Maryland, Massachusetts, New Jersey, New York, and Rhode Island.

Although every state has a CCW permit process, there are certain parts of the United States where private citizens are not allowed to carry concealed weapons. These *No-Issue jurisdiction*s include the District of Columbia, where private citizens typically may not carry handguns in public. Overseas territories such as Puerto Rico, the U.S. Virgin Islands, and American Samoa also are No-Issue jurisdictions. In addition, federal laws prohibit private citizens from carrying handguns on school property or bringing them onto military bases or into federal government buildings, including post offices.

A state-issued CCW permit allows the gun owner to carry his or her weapon in most areas within that state. A gun owner who tries to enter another state where the laws are different may run into trouble. Many states have negotiated *reciprocal agreements*, in which they agree to honor CCW permits issued by the other state. Today, 37 states have reciprocal agreements with at least one other state. Florida, Oklahoma, Alaska, Michigan, and Missouri have the most reciprocal agreements in place with other states. However, before traveling to another state with a handgun, make sure to investigate the laws to determine whether your CCW permit will be honored.

How to Carry a Gun

Most people agree that the best way to carry a gun is in a holster. Holsters are convenient, comfortable, and can protect the finish of your handgun from scratches. Holsters are made from many different types of material, including leather, a type of plastic called Kydex, and heavy nylon fabric.

One thing to keep in mind when purchasing a holster is how it keeps the gun from falling out, or being pulled out by another person. This is known as *retention*. Holsters are rated by their level of retention. Most civilians who carry a concealed handgun use a level 1 holster, which has nothing holding the gun in the holster. This enables them to draw quickly. Military and law enforcement officials often use

If you're planning to carry a concealed weapon, it's important to choose a holster that fits comfortably and also will hold your handgun safely until you need it. A portion of the holster should completely cover and protect the trigger from contact with outside objects, including your finger, until you draw the weapon. A high-quality holster that fits your handgun properly is a worthwhile investment if you plan to carry the gun every day. For a good holster, expect to pay about 10 to 15 percent of the amount you paid for your gun.

A purse is not a good place to carry a handgun for personal defense. It's not easy to draw the weapon quickly, and your handgun can become jammed by small objects in the purse, or dirty. Also, your purse may already be a target for a thief or attacker—if someone grabs it, you won't have access to your gun.

level 2 or 3 holsters. These make it hard for the gun to be pulled out by someone they are struggling to subdue, or to fall out when they are running. A level 2 holster may have a strap that goes over the hand-grip that holds the gun in place, or it may have a trigger guard lock that must be clicked open for the weapon to be drawn. Another form of retention is the thumb break, which is a snap that can be flipped open while the gun is being drawn.

Another thing to evaluate is the *cant*, or angle of the holster relative to the ground. This will determine how easy it is to draw the gun. Some holsters can be canted at various angles, while others are set at a particular angle, usually between 5 and 15 degrees.

A holster can be worn outside the waistband of your pants. Usually these outside the waistband (OWB) holsters are attached to a belt or hooked over the waistband. OWB holsters are harder to hide; they are usually used by police officers and others who are legally allowed to carry a firearm openly in public. Typically, for concealed carrying an inside the waistband (IWB) holster is a better choice.

Many women who carry a handgun will keep it in their purse. However, a purse is not an ideal place for a gun, as it is often filled with small items, such as beads, coins, lint, and pins, that can work their way into a gun and keep it from functioning properly. Also, many women carry other objects in their purse, such as cell phones and makeup, which can make it hard to find the gun when they need it. If you are going to carry a gun in a purse, purchase one that is designed for this purpose. These typically have a special pouch in the back that holds the handgun, so it can be concealed but drawn easily when needed. Some respected makers of concealed carry purses or handbags include Gun Tote'n Mamas, Galco, and Coronado Leathers.

SHOOTING SPORTS

Participating in a competitive shooting sport provides an opportunity to reinforce good shooting habits. There are other benefits as well. At competitive matches, beginners can interact with and learn from more experienced shooters. Plus, competitions are a fun way to spend a day doing something that is enjoyable. The following is some information about the most popular shooting sports for handgun owners.

BULLSEYE: In Bullseye competitions, participants shoot handguns at paper targets hung at fixed distances. Typically, competitors compete in three 90-shot events, using handguns of different calibers. The handguns used are a .22 caliber rimfire, a centerfire handgun of .32 caliber or greater, and a .45 caliber pistol. (You can compete with only two guns, as a centerfire .45 can be used for both the second and third

Bullseye is a great sport for beginners because it provides a solid foundation in core shooting fundamentals—proper aiming, breath control, and trigger pulling. Many people attempt to master Bullseye before moving on to other competitive shooting sports.

events.) Each 90-shot event consists of four matches. The first is known as a "slow-fire" match: 20 shots fired at a six-inch target set at 50 yards with no time restriction. The second is a timed-fire match: five shots (called a "string") in 20 seconds at an eight-inch target set at 25 yards. The strings are done four times for a total of 20 shots. The third match is rapid fire: five shots in 10 seconds at a 25-yard eight-inch target. Again, this is done four times to complete the match. The fourth event is called National Match Course, and includes one 10-shot slow fire string at 50 yards, two five-shot strings of timed fire at 25 yards, and two five-shot strings of rapid fire at 25 yards.

The targets have a series of rings; the outside ring is worth five points, and the inside rings are worth more. The second-smallest ring is worth 10 points. Inside this is a center ring marked with an X; it is also worth 10 points, but is used to break ties when scoring Bullseye events. With three 90-shot events, the highest possible score is 2,700 (270 shots fired in the 10 ring). No one has ever achieved this score in a competition; Hershel Anderson set the world record of 2,680 in 1974. Bullseye is also known as Conventional Pistol Competition.

PLINKING: The term *plinking* refers to informal target shooting, which is often done using non-standard targets such as tin cans, glass bottles, or plastic milk jugs or balloons filled with water. For many years this was the most common way for shooters to practice and improve their skills. For those who live in or near rural areas, it remains much less expensive than regularly

Old cans make ideal targets for plinking. Just be responsible and clean up the mess when you are finished!

shooting at a range. Plus, it's a lot of fun to knock over cans, water bottles, and other targets.

Plinking is sometimes permitted at outdoor shooting ranges. However, it is most commonly done in rural areas without a range master's supervision. Therefore, the shooter must be careful to pick a safe area, keeping in mind the safety rule "Be sure of your target and what is behind it." Bullets can ricochet off rocks or travel farther than intended, so the shooter must consider these possibilities. A good place to plink is usually a large earthen mound to place objects on, in a rural area far away from people, houses, and roads. If there is an earthen hillside a short distance behind the targets to help stop bullets, so much the better.

Even though plinking is an informal shooting experience, responsible shooters should always follow general safety guidelines with regard to handling their firearm. This includes the use of eye and ear protection when shooting.

ISSF EVENTS: The International Shooting Sport Federation (ISSF) sponsors a number of handgun shooting events, as well as competitions for rifle and shotgun shooting. Many of the handgun events are contested using the .22 caliber sport pistol, which must be fired using one hand. Events are held at 50 and 25 meters (roughly 55 and 27 yards). Some events are timed, while others are not. Perhaps the most prestigious of these is the 50 meter pistol event, also known as "free pistol," which has been an Olympic sport since the first Olympic Games was held in 1896. In 50 meter pistol, participants must fire 60 shots from a .22 caliber sport pistol within a maximum time of two hours.

METALLIC SILHOUETTE SHOOTING: A sport that developed in Mexico during the 1930s, Metallic Silhouette Shooting has become popular among many American hunters and sportsmen. It involves shooting at metal targets cut to resemble animals (typically chickens, pigs, turkeys, and rams), which are set at various distances. Handgun matches are held for many different types of weapons: from air pistols to .22 caliber to "big bore" handguns like the .44 caliber and up.

Matches are held for different shooting positions as well; standing and freestyle are options, with targets set at 25, 50, 75, and 100 yards.

In the United States, both the NRA and the International Handgun Metallic Silhouette Association (IHMSA) run competitions in the sport. The International Metallic Silhouette Shooting Union (IMSSU) was formed in 1992 to regulate international competitions in this sport. There are slight differences between international and American competitions.

The IHMSA has a classification system for those who compete in its matches, so that shooters are competing against others who are roughly equal in proficiency. The events are held at gun clubs or ranges that have metallic silhouette courses. The shooters fire at 20 targets (five of each type of animal) per round, with a maximum score of 40 points. Ties are broken by setting up chicken targets (roughly three inches by four inches) at the 100-yard line for a shoot-off.

PRACTICAL SHOOTING: Also known as "action shooting," Practical Shooting is a sport that requires participants to navigate an obstacle-laden course. Speed and accuracy are requirements for success. Practical Shooting began to become popular during the 1960s and 1970s. Today the International Practical Shooting Confederation (IPSC), which oversees the sport, has more than 15,000 members in the United States.

A variation of this sport that has attracted many followers over the past few decades is Cowboy Action Shooting. It combines firearms skill with historical re-enactment, as participants are required to wear Old West costumes and to adopt the persona of a 19th-century Old West figure. The Single Action Shooting Society, which was formed to govern the sport, explained the reason for this in its handbook: "SASS puts a great deal of emphasis on costuming because it adds so much to the uniqueness of our game and helps create a festive, informal atmosphere that supports the friendly, fraternal feeling we encourage in our competitors."

Participants typically must use four guns, all of them similar to firearms that were available in the late 19th century and early 20th

Cowboy Action Shooting is a fun pastime that combines skill in handling firearms available in the 19th century, such as single-action revolvers and lever-action rifles, with historical reenactment.

century. These include two single-action revolvers, a lever-action rifle, and a shotgun. Shooters negotiate a course marked with steel targets as part of a group (called a "posse"). The score is determined by the time it takes to complete the course; missed targets and failing to shoot targets in the proper order add time to the score.

The Single Action Shooting Society (SASS) oversees regional matches conducted by affiliated clubs. It also holds an annual world championship event called End of Trail.

Organizations
to Contact

Gun Owners of America
8001 Forbes Place, Suite 102
Springfield VA 22151
Phone: (703) 321-8585
Fax: (703) 321-8408
Website: www.gunowners.org

**International Handgun
Metallic Silhouette
Association**
P.O. Box 95690
Phone: (801) 733-8423
Fax: (801) 733-8424
Email: Headquarters@ihmsa.org
Website: www.ihmsa.org

**International Practical
Shooting Confederation**
PO Box 972
Oakville, Ontario
Canada L6K 0B1
Phone: (208) 978-2898
Email: info@ipsc.org
Website: www.ipsc.org

**National Association of
Certified Firearms Instructors**
Tim Grant, President
4722 Forest Circle
Minnetonka, MN 55345
Phone: (952) 935-2414
Email: info@nacfi.us
Website: www.nacfi.us

National Rifle Association
11250 Waples Mill Road
Fairfax, VA 22030
Phone: (800) 672-3888
Fax (703) 267-3989
Website: www.nra.org

**National Shooting Sports
Foundation**
Flintlock Ridge Office Center
11 Mile Hill Road
Newtown, CT 06470
Phone: (203) 426-1320
Fax: (203) 426-1087
Website: www.nssf.org

Glossary

action—the mechanism of a handgun that presents a cartridge for firing; when the gun is fired it also removes the spent shell casing and introduces a fresh cartridge.

ballistics—the science of cartridge discharge and a bullet's flight.

barrel—the long tubular part of a firearm, which provides direction and velocity for the bullet. The interior of a gun barrel is sometimes referred to as the bore.

breech—the part of a gun that contains the rear chamber portion of the barrel, action, trigger or firing mechanism, and the magazine.

bullet—the metal projectile expelled from the cartridge when a handgun is fired.

caliber—the diameter of the bore of a gun barrel, usually measured in tenths of an inch or in millimeters.

cartridge—ammunition consisting of a brass case, primer, smokeless powder, and a projectile.

centerfire—a cartridge in which the primer or primer assembly is seated in a pocket or recess in the center of the base of the brass casing; this term also refers to a firearm that uses centerfire cartridges.

chamber—the part of a firearm at the rear of the barrel where the cartridge is placed before firing.

cock—to draw the hammer back against its spring until it becomes latched against the sear, or sometimes the trigger itself. Once cocked, the hammer will be released by a subsequent pull of the trigger.

cylinder—a rotating chamber in a revolver that typically holds five or six cartridges. The cylinder is linked to the firing mechanism, so that a new chamber is rotated into alignment with the barrel each time the revolver is fired.

double-action—a revolver or pistol on which a long trigger pull can both cock and release the hammer to fire the weapon.

firing pin—in a hammer-fired gun, this is a hardened pin housed in the breechblock, centered directly behind the primer cap of a chambered cartridge. When struck by the hammer it impacts the primer cap of the cartridge, discharging the weapon.

frame—the main body of a handgun to which the action, barrel, and grip are connected.

grip—the handle used to hold a handgun.

magazine—a device that holds multiple ammunition cartridges under spring pressure, so they can be rapidly fed into a handgun's chamber.

misfire—a condition when firing a gun in which a cartridge fails to discharge.

muzzle—the forward end of the barrel where the projectile exits.

pistol—any handgun that is not a revolver.

primer—explosive material that, when struck by a handgun's firing pin, ignites the charge of smokeless powder in a cartridge.

rifling—a series of spiral grooves cut into the bore of a gun barrel. Rifling stabilizes a bullet in flight by causing it to spin. Rifling may rotate to the right or left.

rimfire—a type of cartridge in which the primer is contained inside the hollow rim of the case. The primer is detonated by the firing pin striking the outside edge of the rim, crushing the rim against the rear face of the barrel.

safety—a mechanical device built into a handgun that prevents it from being fired inadvertently or accidentally.

sear—part of a gun's action that catches and holds the hammer when it is cocked. Pressure on the trigger causes the sear to release the hammer, allowing it to strike the firing pin and discharge the weapon.

single-action—a type of pistol or revolver in which the trigger is only used for firing the weapon, and cannot be used to cock the firing mechanism. The hammer must be manually pulled back before a shot can be fired.

slide—part of the action of a semi-automatic pistol. It slides along tracks in the top of the frame during the recoil process, allowing spent shells to be ejected and moving a new cartridge from the magazine into the chamber.

trigger—part of the firing system that, when pulled by the shooter's index finger, activates the hammer.

Further Reading

Ayoob, Massad. *Greatest Handguns of the World*. Iola, Wis.: F + W Media, Inc., 2010.

Bussard, Michael E. *NRA Firearms Sourcebook: Your Ultimate Guide to Guns, Ballistics, and Shooting*. Fairfax, Va.: National Rifle Association, 2006.

Cunningham, Grant. *Gun Digest Shooter's Guide to Handguns*. Iola, Wis.: F + W Media, Inc., 2012.

Gregersen, Steven D. *The Gun Guide for Those Who Know Nothing About Firearms*. New York: CreateSpace, 2012.

Leghorn, Nick. *Getting Started with Firearms in the United States: A Complete Guide for Newbies*. New York: CreateSpace, 2012.

Lyons, Larry. *The Gun Owner's Handbook: A Complete Guide to Maintaining and Repairing Your Firearms in the Field or at Your Workbench*. Guilford, Conn.: The Lyons Press, 2006.

NRA Education and Training Division. *NRA Guide to the Basics of Pistol Shooting*. Fairfax, Va.: National Rifle Association, 2009.

Rementer, Stephen R., and Bruce N. Eimer. *The Essential Guide to Handguns: Firearm Instruction for Personal Defense and Protection*. Flushing, N.Y.: Looseleaf Law Press, 2005.

Steier, David. *Guns 101: A Beginner's Guide to Buying and Owning Firearms*. New York: Skyhorse Publishing, 2011.

Internet Resources

http://www.boone-crockett.org

Boone and Crockett Club is an organization that promotes wildlife conservation and hunter safety. It was founded by Theodore Roosevelt in 1887, making it the oldest such organization in the United States.

http://www.nssf.org/safety

The National Shooting Sports Foundation's web page on firearm safety includes educational videos and articles about safe and responsible gun ownership.

http://www.nraila.org/gun-laws/state-laws.aspx

At this site, the NRA maintains a state-by-state listing of gun laws related to firearms ownership.

http://www.handgunlaw.us

This site is regularly updated with information about state and federal statutes related to firearm ownership.

http://www.nrainstructors.org/searchcourse.aspx

This searchable database enables you to find a certified NRA shooting and safety instructor in your local area.

Index

Numbers in **bold italic** refer to captions.

About the Author

John Cashin served as a military policeman in the U.S. Army, and recently retired after 20 years as a police officer in South Carolina. An avid hunter and outdoorsman, he owns several handguns, including a .22 target pistol and a .357 magnum. He lives near McCormick, South Carolina, with his wife Elizabeth. This is his second book.